Because Life Be Lifing

Emery J. Cannon, CPC.

Copyright © 2024 Emery J. Cannon

All rights reserved.

ISBN: 9798340064356

DEDICATION

This book is dedicated to those who have committed themselves to becoming a better version of who they are. Every day, we face obstacles and naturally overcome them. Congratulations on already being great. I hope this book helps you realize that everything you need is already inside of YOU.

CONTENTS

Acknowledgments   i

Introduction   1

The Early Years   3

The Teen Years   10

The Twenties   20

The Thirties   28

The Forties   37

Life   44

Because Life Be Lifing   47

About the Author   50

INTRODUCTION

The goal of this book is to motivate those who need motivation, inspire those who seek to aspire, and overcome objections in their simplest form. Life is ever-changing, and the only way to succeed in both personal and business aspects is to be prepared. The objective is to always be a lifelong learner and never repeat the same mistakes. Take only the best of what you learn and apply it every day. The last thing we want is to keep learning the same lessons over and over again. It takes away from our time and purpose.

I intend to take you down memory lane and show you two results. The first is your willingness to grow, and the second is your willingness to learn. These are natural for us, as they are embedded in us as humans. We must adhere to our most natural and pure selves to grow into what our purpose will become. Big dreams only become reality when you decide you want them.

Our purpose is what drives us. We must at least understand what we are meant for and where we perform best. Not everyone is here to be a rock star, billionaire, or actor. The people who interact with you every day can have the greatest impact on you. For example, Madonna may have been your favorite artist, but the nurse who wrapped your arm in bandages after you fell off the swing may be your true source of motivation.

Ultimately, the path to overcoming life's daily objections is rooted in self-awareness, growth, and purpose. We are capable of achieving greatness when we stop looking outside for validation and realize that the power to overcome is already within us. Embrace your journey, honor your lessons, and move forward with the confidence that you can conquer any obstacle. Remember: the world isn't changed by those who wait, but by those who take action with the belief that they are enough. You already have everything you need to succeed—now, it's time to use it.

THE EARLY YEARS

Let's start at the very beginning, where life and learning truly commence. Since the moment we were born, our survival instincts and critical thinking kicked in. Even before we could form words or understand the world around us, we were already driven by the need to survive and ensure our basic needs were met. We had to breathe, cry, and communicate in the only ways we knew how, hoping to get what we needed. This was the foundation of our existence, and it underscores one of the most powerful qualities we possess as humans: the ability to adapt. We were born to adapt, and that skill is what ensures our survival.

I know starting here opens up Pandora's box, especially for those whose beginnings weren't easy. But no matter how difficult your start was, the fact that you're here now means you adapted. That's not something to be taken lightly. Whether your life was filled with support or adversity, one constant remains: you found a way forward. And that's a testament to the resilience that exists within every one of us. As humans, we're built to overcome. We grow, evolve, and persevere, regardless of the circumstances we're born into.

It's important to acknowledge that not everyone had their basic needs met as children. Some of us lacked the nurturing environment others took for granted. But even in those cases, where support and care were scarce, that wasn't the end of the story. It was simply the beginning of a more challenging journey. For children who didn't have the safety nets others did, it became crucial to adapt quickly, to learn how to survive on their own terms. A lack of nurture and support doesn't mean a dead end; it simply accelerates the need for growth and resilience.

As children, we constantly faced challenges, and we overcame them. From rolling over for the first time to taking our first steps, these might seem like small moments now, but back then, they were monumental. They were victories. And the reason we often take them for granted is that everything around us, even as children, influenced us. Those influences—whether from family, caregivers, or the world at large—were so constant and omnipresent that we almost subconsciously expected certain milestones to happen. Yet, those first steps and challenges were no small feat. They were the first examples of our ability to adapt to life's ever-changing landscape.

If you think back, you'll likely remember the first time you accomplished something unexpected. Maybe it was a small victory—something no one else even noticed—but to you, it felt monumental. How did it make you feel? That rush of pride, that sense of achievement—that's what success feels like. And as humans, we chase that feeling. It's not just success that we pursue; we also long for security, hope, love, and acceptance. These core feelings are embedded in our experiences from childhood and continue to drive us throughout our lives.

It's incredible how much of what we accomplish as adults is rooted in those early years. The challenges we faced back then helped shape the person we are today. Some tasks were easy, revealing natural talents we didn't even know we had. Others were harder, pushing us to the point where we needed help from others. That's where we learned the value of asking for assistance, of leaning on those around us. I was challenged many times as a child, whether it was in school, sports, or even completing simple chores at home. And I vividly remember how those moments made me feel. Whether it was the pride of success or the sting of failure, each one of those experiences shaped me.

I can still recall playing baseball as a kid and missing a ball that came straight toward me. It was frustrating—I had practiced so much, and yet, in the moment that mattered, I didn't succeed. At the time, it felt like the end of the world. But now, looking back, I see how that failure helped me grow. It wasn't just about missing the ball; it was about learning to cope with setbacks and understanding that failure is part of the journey. On the flip side, I also remember the time I caught a pop fly. The feeling of triumph in that moment was indescribable. I was on top of the world, filled with pride and accomplishment. These contrasting experiences—failure and success—are what help us develop resilience and a deeper understanding of ourselves.

Our parents and guardians played significant roles in guiding us through these early years, though their ability to do so often depended on how well they navigated their own lives. One thing we come to realize as we grow older is that while advice is always valuable, its source matters. As children, we don't have the discernment to know whether the advice we receive is sound, but as we mature, we learn to critically evaluate the wisdom offered to us. The truth is, no one person is an expert at everything. We must learn to identify who in our lives is best equipped to guide us, based on their experiences, expertise, and understanding of our specific situations.

Life is full of hurdles, and how we handle those challenges often depends on how we were raised. Disappointment is inevitable in childhood, but it's also character-building. One of the most significant challenges we face as children is making friends. Do you remember your first friend? That moment when you found someone who understood you, someone you connected with, was incredibly validating. It made you feel accepted, seen, and valued. That sense of acceptance is something we seek out for the rest of our lives, and it's rooted in those early experiences.

As children, we were constantly adapting to new challenges. One of the biggest hurdles we had to face was school. School is more than just a place to learn; it's a battleground for social acceptance, academic achievement, and personal growth. The early school years—grades K-5—are some of the most critical in shaping who we become. During this time, we start to discover where our strengths lie and where we struggle. Some of us grasp concepts quickly, while others need more time to catch on. That's normal.

I've experienced all three categories: understanding things right away, struggling to get it, and sometimes not getting it at all. Some children, the ones who seem to understand everything immediately, have a smoother path when it comes to academics. But that doesn't mean they don't face challenges in other areas. I often admired my classmates who seemed to breeze through their studies while I struggled with certain subjects. While I excelled in areas like social studies and math, I watched in awe as others consistently earned top marks in every subject.

For those of us who didn't grasp information as quickly, there was often a temptation to cover up our struggles by acting out or becoming a distraction. I know this because I did it myself. Rather than risk being called on and answering a question incorrectly, I would sometimes create a disturbance to avoid embarrassment. It was a defense mechanism, a way to protect myself from failure. But it was also a hurdle I needed to overcome.

Over time, I realized that this behavior stemmed from fear — fear of the unknown and fear of failure. But here's the thing: fear is just another obstacle. It's something we can overcome if we face it head-on. Most children, even if they don't realize it at the time, will eventually adapt and find a way to succeed. It may not happen at the same pace for everyone, but the key is to keep moving forward. Small wins in those early years build the confidence needed to tackle larger challenges later in life.

It's also important to recognize that not everyone processes information at the same speed. Some students need extra help to catch up, and that's perfectly normal. This is where the role of a great teacher comes in. A teacher who understands the unique needs of each student can help guide them through the learning process, ensuring that no one is left behind. But sometimes, students slip through the cracks, and that's when parents need to step in. When a child is struggling, it's essential to intervene early to ensure they receive the support they need.

As I mentioned earlier, the harder a task is, the more fear it can generate in a child. That fear is often compounded by two factors: natural competitiveness and the desire for acceptance. We are, by nature, competitive beings. We want to succeed, and we want to be accepted by our peers. As children, this drive is even stronger. Every child wants to be good at something, whether it's academics, sports, or creative pursuits. And once they identify their strength, they're eager to compete and prove themselves.

For example, I had a friend who was unbeatable at the video game Tecmo Bowl. He played it thousands of times, and I may have beaten him only twice. He excelled at that game, just as I excelled at basketball. We each had our strengths, and we took pride in them. That's what childhood is about—discovering your strengths and using them to build confidence.

I've seen this process unfold many times. I remember a basketball player from my grade school who was incredibly talented. She was the MVP of our team and consistently scored half of our points. She went on to play at a nationally ranked high school, but by her junior year, she lost interest and decided to focus on her studies. The pressure had taken the joy out of the game for her. On the flip side, I knew a classmate who had never played sports before, but with the encouragement of his coach, he became the star of the football team by his junior year.

Being great at something builds confidence, and that confidence spills over into every area of a child's life. You can see it in the way they speak, the way they participate, and the way they carry themselves. It's a powerful thing to watch a child develop self-esteem and belief in their abilities.

Looking back, it's inspiring to see how much children overcome in those early years—whether it's learning to add and subtract, mastering grammar, or simply forming complete sentences. It's equally rewarding when they ask for help and you can guide them toward achieving their goals. When children learn that overcoming obstacles is a natural part of life, they begin to develop strategies for handling future challenges. The more experiences they have, the more tools they gather for the road ahead. These early strategies sharpen their skills and prepare them for even greater success as young adults and beyond.

THE TEEN YEARS

The teen years are the most difficult transformation years. They're critical for development throughout these years. There are so many obstacles we overcome during our teens: Physical Development, Emotional Development, Intellectual Development, and, most importantly to a teen, Social Development. The reality is that life is always "lifing," throwing us experiences we never saw coming, and it's during these teen years that we start to realize that fact.

Let's talk about the obvious when it comes to teens. Physical change is normally the most important to teens. When I was a teen, I remember being caught up in height and worried about weight. Mainly weight, because most of my peers had a smaller build, and I had a larger build with broad shoulders. I always felt bigger because I was bigger. When we shopped for clothes, I always had to go to the husky section of the store. Why couldn't they just make my size in the men's section or kids' section? Why did it have to say husky? I can remember other classmates at the same store in other sections, and I was in my own section trying on clothes because of my size. I'm not sure when that complex went away, but it didn't last long going into my freshman year in high school.

I felt lucky because my size and weight never hindered my physical ability. I was able to run and play sports with all of the physically fit kids. But even though my body caught up—my height evened out, and my broad shoulders didn't seem to matter as much—it taught me something about life's unpredictability. Life just be lifing in its own way, changing us when we least expect it. At one point, I felt self-conscious, and at another point, I was comfortable in my own skin. As a child, being bigger didn't matter much because kids aren't as cruel with their words, but as you go into high school, your looks and physique become the highlight of most conversations.

Emotions run high in teens, and looks are a very high priority in their lifestyle. You can find most teens in the bathroom or a bedroom with a phone or a picture, normally looking at themselves because, in the era we live in, with social media, it is important to them. Even before social media and camera phones, it was important. Teens care about how they look to others. Depending on their social group, their style, language, and peers will differ. Things haven't changed much when it comes to grouping for teens. There is always the cool group, athletic group, intellectual group, aware group, and chill group. Inside these groups, there are always teens who relate to other groups and feel out of place in the group they're in. That creates crossover groups, which help create parties!

I mention all of this for two reasons. The first is to give you a reminder of some of the awkwardness of being a teen. Second, you can see how much you had to overcome as a teen. Life was "lifing" back then too—it just looked a bit different. It was life unfolding in ways we weren't fully ready for, but we adapted to it nonetheless. I talk to clients about this era in their life; some are extremely sensitive, and some thought it was the glory days. Some clients tell me they would love to get back to the physical shape they were in then versus now, and others feel like they're in the best shape of their life right now. Either way, both sides agree it helped mold them into who they are today.

Emotional Development

Emotional development for teens varies in so many ways. During their teens, the emotional experience can go from one extreme of being super high and very emotional to super low and close to depressive. The reason for this variation is because during these most crucial years of development, they are trying to learn to understand themselves and how to express themselves. The teen years are a time when life starts to show you how it can be both beautiful and overwhelming—life starts "lifing" in ways we aren't prepared for.

In the past few years, mental awareness and mental health have been a priority amongst young people, which has given education to those who seek to learn about themselves and their condition. Before recent years, either information was scarce, or no one knew about true mental health and awareness. As a teen, we were all so different, and then there were those who we thought were strange. Understanding that everyone is not the same, and we are all different because we are not all raised the same and all have different motivators that influence us, is important. Emotional development comes from a combination of home and outside influences.

We begin to see that life is always moving, pushing, pulling, and shaping us, and we are learning how to deal with it. This is the essence of what "lifing" really is—whether it's the small emotional ups and downs or bigger moments of self-discovery, we're learning how to ride those waves, even if we don't realize it.

How do we begin to talk about emotional development? First, we have to ask ourselves, what is emotional development? It involves learning what feelings and emotions are, understanding how and why they occur, recognizing your own feelings and those of others, and developing effective ways for managing those feelings. Now the question is, how does this work in teens? The simple answer is finding a process of gradually increasing the ability to perceive, assess, and manage emotions. The natural order of life is to gradually accept our emotions as a teen. It spikes from one end of the spectrum to the other, and we never understand why. That is the world balancing itself by waiting until you're old enough to start to reason with it but young enough to begin life as an adult.

When I was a teen, I found myself questioning my place in the lives of people close to me. I felt like I wanted to know where I ranked. This was always my question to people like my grandmother, my great-grandmother, my aunts, my uncles, and my cousins. I'm not sure why, but it was important for me to know the answer. I remember so vividly me asking, and everybody laughing at me, asking why I wanted to know. I felt emotionally I wanted to matter to someone, and also I was just nosey. I learned later that may have been my fear of not being loved as much as others.

I overcame that fear and that question as I got older, as we all do as time goes on and we become more secure in our emotions and feelings. I actually never thought to ask the question again as I grew into my middle teens. Life "lifed" on me during those years. It showed me that emotional balance doesn't come easy, but it does come with time. Teens have insecurities, and we all have to have them fulfilled. The end result is that emotional development for teens is all over the place, and we need this time in our lives to learn how to balance and learn ourselves. This is the perfect time because we are maturing into adulthood, and we can prioritize our emotional development.

Once we have accomplished the balance of our emotions, our purpose becomes clear. We are able to make educated decisions and understand why we came to the conclusion. This creates less peer pressure and more individual thinking. We learn to navigate how life be "lifing" emotionally, and with that, we grow.

Intellectual Development

The next stage of development as a teen is intellectual development. During the teen years, if you can remember, we start to formulate and develop the difference between logical and possible thinking. When I talk about logical thinking for a teen, I am speaking of learning to understand complex thinking skills. How a child may view the world is different because of a lack of information, but as you go into adolescence, your view becomes different because you have experienced more and understand more of societal standards to a degree. The teen is able to start long-term thinking about the world and even find their place at that time where they want to be. They start to formulate questions like, why do I have to do the dishes, whereas before they saw you doing the dishes and wanted to help.

As they develop and formulate opinions, it's based off the same principles of the social environment. I can remember going with my mom at the end of the school year to help her clear out her classroom when I was just a child, and when we were done with her class, she would send me to other teachers, and I would run to each classroom and happily help and be just as happy and smiling. When I became a teen, I was asked to do the same as I had always done for years before, but the older I became, the more I wondered why I had to help everybody. I asked, when your room is cleaned out, can't we just leave? Her question to me was, why wouldn't I help people who didn't have help? I didn't know why, so I would help her colleagues. It was a great question she asked me, but when I was a child, it never crossed my mind to ask.

Teens begin to intellectualize life differently. It's not just about emotions; it's about problem-solving. As we grow, life "lifes" on us intellectually too. We're faced with challenges that we couldn't foresee and problems we don't yet have the tools to solve. This is where we begin to learn how to face life logically, step by step.

We start to have small wins in different stages of our life. For instance, receiving an A or numerous A's on a report card, winning a spelling bee, or even getting an accolade in sports. All of this success builds confidence. It shows us we can overcome and succeed. While overcoming obstacles as a teen, the experiences we go through help create our view of the world. Everything we go through creates our vision of the world. We don't all see the same picture. Our perception is based on our reality. Our reality is our experience.

Learning to listen versus using physical answers is another challenge. As we get older, we start to develop a sense of listening, but it's hard. We've just learned to think for ourselves, and now we have to consider others' perspectives. Learning to listen with an open mind takes time, but it's a key part of growing.

Social Development

The final section of teen development is social development. As a teen, social development is normally broken down into a space of ages. For example, a 13-year-old will have different milestones than a 16-year-old. At 13, a teen is starting to make personal decisions by defining themselves through the different influences of everyday life. They are starting to develop independence, influences, sexual identity, and most importantly, values.

Remember, at 13, they are still in the beginning stages, so some of these characteristics won't be permanent. This is a teen defining themselves and expressing themselves. I can remember at 13, I was conflicted with wanting to identify as a wrestler and boxer. We set up our backyard with four logs in a square to have a ring. We made heavyweight belts out of aluminum foil and cardboard. In our neighborhood, we rounded up around 8 to 10 guys and had matches every day. We were really wrestling and really getting hurt, but it was exciting and fun while it lasted. This is totally opposite of my best friend, who identified as a baseball player and basketball player because sports were his scope of influence. He played both sports and ran track. He kept stats of major league players and NBA players. There was no stat about any player he didn't already know. He did well in every sport. He found his purpose early.

It's the balance of life. Creating a space where you have independence but also have friends, family, and social acquaintances. At 13, they won't have these things completely figured out, but it is the beginning stages of learning how to create the space and develop it. Previously, you only really mixed with friends from events, family, and assigned friends. Now they are making the decision about who and when they choose to divide their time. This is not only a big adjustment for them but also for others in their life who originally took priority.

As they begin to understand these characteristics, they also start to become part of a culture. The culture is created by the influences in their environment. Their influences include people, places, and things. All around their city, on the radio, on television, in music, and school. All of this defines how they will be influenced. I have found this to be true no matter what city I go to in the world. I look around many cities, and when you go to the malls and halls of schools, you see what the city or township's influences are, and it is embedded in its inhabitants.

At age 16, a lot of the unsure thoughts are almost dispelled, and your teen is molding more and more into a young adult. They have a better sense of self-esteem and a better idea of who they are and what they want without doubting their decisions. To be clear, that does not mean that they are ready or even close to being 100 percent correct. It does give them a sense of awareness and belonging in society. At this age, we understand that we are walking into adulthood. I remember being 16 and understanding that I felt like I should be independent and wanting to own a business or at least be related to being in a business. I knew this back then. I'm not saying at 16 you know exactly what you want to be in life, but I knew I wasn't going to be a wrestler by then.

What a difference those three years made. My influences were different, and not because I knew any business owners. It was because of what I didn't see, which was business owners in my circle of influences. That was always my motivation—to do what I didn't see others doing. As we all know, there are always roadblocks to get to any goal at all ages. I started out working in a real job at Hardee's, a fast-food restaurant. Far from being a businessman. What I didn't know then, but I do now, is that all roads lead to your pathway. I learned a lot working at Hardee's, including learning how to spend money. I learned how to budget. Once I got my first job, my first lesson from my mom was to pay for the things that I needed and wanted. I paid for my clothes, my food, and all my extra activities. If I overspent my funds from my paycheck, then I had no money. I learned that by my second check. I learned to put my needs before my wants immediately. I learned to factor in known and unknown costs so that I could budget until I got paid again. I also learned how to pay myself and put money aside so that I could purchase bigger items and not struggle after the purchase.

From ages 16 to 18, they are working on understanding the rules of life. They are looking for independence. Right before your eyes, they are starting to be lifing.

Being a teen is so amazing. Learning how to become a functioning adult is an adventure. Learning to overcome life's objections at such a small scale and with limited liability. Going through these phases during your teens helps prepare you for the real challenges that may come. Overcoming physical development, emotional development, intellectual development, and social development. These are all natural developments. Each one helping us become better decision makers. Look at all we have overcome to this point. We have conquered all of these natural developments by gaining experience in troubleshooting current problems.

As teens, the problems come, and we give our best judgment to solve them without any experience. If it was a successful outcome, we learn how to handle that problem. If it was unsuccessful, we learn not to do that again. Whether we are trying to decide if our body is too big or too small and being self-conscious about it either way or trying to decide how to categorize a friendship, we learn to adapt and overcome at early ages. What a great time to learn as we enter into some of the biggest moments of our lives, all while life keeps on lifing.

THE TWENTIES

This is it—the beginning stages of adulthood. This is where adulthood begins, and childhood ends. We are not done learning lessons; in fact, we are about to embark on some of the greatest lessons that life can teach us. Whether you decide to seek an education after high school, pursue a trade, or go straight into the workforce, the lessons will add up the same. During this time period, we start to find Maturity, Consequences, Careers, and Independence. All the lessons we learned in our teens have brought us to these developmental milestones, and trust me – life will be "lifing" hard in your twenties, throwing more unexpected twists and turns your way. There are plenty of other skills we will learn throughout our twenties, but as a whole, these are the skills we all get the opportunity to go through.

What does maturity look like in our twenties? Well, for one, we have to develop self-control. As adults, our actions and words have to change—no more tantrums. We have to learn to control our emotions versus letting them control us. As children, things were "unfair." I remember always using that word, "unfair," and at the time, I thought it was true. Maturing means realizing nothing in life is truly fair. We all have different backgrounds. Just like we all have points of view, in reverse, everyone will have one of you and treat you according to that point of view. Is it fair because they don't know you? Absolutely not, but it is up to you to change that viewpoint. Going into adulthood is not about fairness, but more about how you can control the things within your control. No situation will be perfect, but making the best out of the situation is the best outcome.

In your twenties, you will always be perceived as having a lack of experience or not enough drive. Every generation goes through these phases. The baby boomers think everybody is lazy and has no self-control. Generation X thinks they are resourceful and independent. Gen Y or millennials are known for being tech-savvy, diverse, and socially conscious. But one thing is true for every generation: adapting to an ever-changing life. How you handle it will define your growth. Controlling emotions and words isn't easy, but as you gain experience, it becomes more natural. You start thinking before you speak because life teaches you the importance of consequences.

How will I do this, you ask? You will start making thoughtful decisions. You will start thinking before you speak. Now, this will not happen the day you turn twenty. It will come together for you as you start to see the consequences of not thinking ahead. Whether you pursue college, trade school, or jump into the workforce, success in your twenties will require you to master self-control. It's the key to weathering the unpredictability of life.

I remember early in my twenties, fresh into the Army, I lacked self-control, and my squad paid for it. I recall one of my first weeks in basic training, talking back to the drill sergeant after a long, exhausting day. Not only was I punished, but so was my entire squad. We were up all night doing push-ups, sit-ups, and running. I wasn't mad at the drill sergeants because I knew it was their job to train us. I will tell you this: I have never had a problem being responsible for my own consequences, but to punish an entire squad because of my lack of self-control made me think a little harder about my motivation and what I could do to control myself.

The world doesn't change much from the military to civilian life. There is structure, beginnings, and endings everywhere. Life will always be lifing—throwing you challenges and opportunities in equal measure. The key is knowing that if you start something, you must finish it. That takes commitment, self-control, and decision-making—qualities you will develop as life keeps lifing.

When we go into adulthood, we quickly learn about

consequences. Consequences are the effect, result, or outcome of something occurring earlier. Everything you do right now has an effect later. There are good consequences as well as learning consequences. There will always be an outcome to everything you do in life. Even if you do nothing, there will be a result from that as well. When you least expect it, the consequences of your actions will catch up with you—sometimes immediately, sometimes years down the line. Always do your best in determining how a decision could affect you later in life. As we navigate into adulthood, our consequences become more real, more important, and more crucial to how our future will be determined.

I remember being 19 and joining the Army. I had no idea how much that decision would shape my future. Serving my full term and getting out honorably opened doors I never imagined. Life be lifing in ways we don't expect, but it also opens new paths. Veterans get great opportunities in the workplace, which helped me secure jobs when it was time to transition back into civilian life. My only goal for joining the Army was to see more of the world and get out of St. Louis. But life had a bigger plan for me, and I reaped far more benefits than I expected.

But life doesn't just throw you positive consequences. In my early twenties, I was a heavy eater and drinker, and as a result, I developed diabetes. This diagnosis had a huge impact on my health and my daily life. Life really lifes like that—sometimes it throws challenges that force you to change. Diabetes taught me to manage my health, control my diet, and exercise regularly. Life threw me a curveball, and I had to learn how to adapt. That's the thing about your twenties—you learn to navigate obstacles, and how you do it determines your future.

When you're in your twenties, the idea of a career is often the furthest thing from your mind. Sure, a job is important, but few people are thinking about their lifelong career at 21. After my time in the Army, I had no clue what was next for me. I was reading the paper and saw an ad for a car salesman job that was paying $2,500 a month. At the time, it sounded like an amazing salary. I woke up early the next morning, put on a shirt, tie, and some slacks, and drove to the address. It said Jim Reed Chevrolet. I walked in, very nervous because I had no clue what to expect. I asked for Brandon Mosley, the name in the paper. This guy was energetic and excited, and I was nervous as well as excited. He asked me a few questions and said, "I like you, kid." He sent me to the next interview with the truck manager. This guy was even more energetic than the last, moving forward and backward, left to right, talking about trucks and sales without missing a beat. I was in amazement. He did the same thing—asked me a few questions—and before I knew it, he shouted, "Follow me." I thought he was walking me to my car. Before I knew it, I was in the General Manager's office, sitting down, talking to Steve Brink.

Remember when I said being in the military opened doors for me that may not have been opened otherwise? This was one of those doors. It turned out Steve had served in the Navy and was only hiring one guy to start selling cars at this 70-plus-year-old dealership. Steve hired me on the spot after a two-hour conversation. I felt honored to be among such an honorable dealership with such an amazing history. The military experience I didn't think much of ended up opening doors for me, and just like that, I fell into a career that's now spanned over 22 years.

According to the data, most entry-level careers start between the ages of 20 and 25. So this is the decade when you start to find out what you like, what you're good at, and what you have an interest in when it comes to a career. I'm not saying you will stay in this field forever, because you may not like where you initially start. I am saying by the time you hit your twenties, you are gauging what you want to do for income. You are also finding a fit for yourself—a place where your values and work ethic align with the company. If you are coming out of college, you've picked a path, and now you have to link your path with your principles.

I learned later in life that when you are being interviewed, make sure you are doing a little investigating yourself to ensure you will be appreciated for the dedication you are about to offer. About three years after being hired at Jim Reed Chevrolet, I was approached by their competition across the street and was offered a promotion into finance and my own office with a bathroom. I took the offer and went to the other dealership. It only took a week, but I could see the disorganization and mayhem going on in the dealership. After a month, I wished I had never taken the offer. I'm not sure if it was divine intervention, but the owner of Jim Reed Chevrolet called me and asked to meet with me. Mr. Reed asked me if I was ready to come back home. I said, "Absolutely." He looked at me and said, "All you had to do was ask." I started back at Jim Reed Chevrolet the next day. I did not investigate the competition enough, and I found out there were other benefits that were important to me besides money and a bathroom in my office.

I wasn't looking for a career. I was looking to feed my family, and it turned into a career. I could have just as easily stayed in the military and enjoyed a career. My biggest point is that in our early twenties, you think you're on one path, and suddenly, you're rerouted. Opportunities arise in unexpected places, and a simple job can turn into a career if you follow where life takes you. But remember, just because you start a career in one field doesn't mean you'll stay there forever. Life keeps lifing, and it's okay to change direction when it feels right. For instance, I have a great friend who studied to be a teacher, got her degree, took her test, and taught high school students for six years. In her seventh year, she took a look and decided that teaching wasn't the best fit for her. She went back to school to become a nurse practitioner, and she has enjoyed that career for 11 years now.

Just because you start a career in one field doesn't mean you will do that forever. I tell my clients over and over to never limit your opportunities—we are life learners.

We are adults now; it's time to start adulting. Part of adulting (yes, adulting—I know this is not a real word) is gaining freedom or a lack of freedom—we call it independence. Independence is another major part of your twenties. Independence sounds amazing—freedom to come and go as you please, being the boss of your own life. But the flip side is responsibility. Life be lifing hard when you realize independence means bills, obligations, and no safety net. Whether it's your first apartment or moving into a dorm, the responsibility of taking care of yourself becomes real. All the behind-the-scenes duties your parents or guardians used to handle for you have now become your responsibility.

It sounds great going through the process, and it feels great to say it in the beginning, but I quickly found out this was a little more than my mother let on when I was growing up. You will have to adjust quickly because when your new life starts, it doesn't stop. The bills don't stop, the grocery shopping doesn't stop, and the responsibility grows as your needs grow. This is all part of becoming an adult. If done correctly, you will always want more out of life, and this will only be a stepping stone to success.

Life really moves in stages to get you ready for the next step. I went from working at Hardee's making $4.25 an hour living at home with my mother to entering the Army making about $25,000 a year living in barracks to selling cars in a career, all before I turned 30 years old. Look how far you have come in life. Can you remember your first job? Do you remember the starting wage? At what age did you gain your independence? I always tell people I didn't gain independence for myself until I left the military because I feel I still had a cushion in the Army. When I got out of the Army, I had to really explore life. I had to find an apartment, turn on utilities, and buy food weekly. All of that was provided by Uncle Sam.

I can still remember my first apartment. It was $900 a month in Lebanon, Tennessee. I had a 3-bedroom and 2-bathroom apartment. It was perfect for my little family at the time. It was 1,000 square feet of independence, and in my second month, the reality of adulthood hit me. Bills, rent, groceries—it all added up fast. The bills started coming in, and I had to learn how to budget. That $2,500 started dwindling down quickly. Lucky for me, this new job in sales as a car salesman had incentives to make more money—called commission checks. The more cars I sold, the more commission I received. I learned then that I would go to work and give this job the very best I had to offer so that I could make more money. I did very well in this industry throughout my twenties.

We all grow into our careers. The longer we do it and learn the process, the better we progress and develop our skills. Whether we choose to bartend, work on an assembly line, drive a forklift, work in sales, or work in healthcare, we will evolve and become great if we evolve.

When you make life decisions in your twenties, they will affect your thirties and forties as well. Look how far you have come, from learning your basic needs as a child to conquering physical, emotional, intellectual, and social developmental skills, to becoming an adult and tackling real-life problems. Learning maturity, learning about consequences, learning where you fit with your purpose and career, and finally, gaining independence. You have tackled so much, and you are just at the beginning of adulthood. We still have more to learn as life learners. We still have more to gain. We still have more to give as humans. Life never stops lifing—it's an ongoing journey. But as we walk into our thirties, we do so knowing that each challenge has prepared us for the next step. Life be lifing, but we'll be ready for it.

THE THIRTIES

In our thirties, we start to apply everything we have learned up to now. By the time we hit our thirties, we have had the opportunity to gain experience. We have made some great decisions, some terrible decisions, and done some valuable learning. The truth is, life doesn't stop "lifing" just because we've hit another milestone—it actually tends to throw even more our way. What can we expect to gain from all this exposure? First, we become aware of what we've learned. Did we make terrible decisions because we lacked knowledge, experience, or education? Then we must evaluate the problem and decide what we could have done to change the outcome to be positive. These are skills we possess in our thirties because our minds are able to problem-solve more clearly. And that's crucial because as we all know, life is going to keep "lifing." The great thing about being life learners is that we still have more development we can add to our journey that will equip us with more tools to be a more complete and driven force.

What we learn in our thirties is awareness of ourselves. We don't actually look at it as learning awareness—it's one of those natural processes we develop as we age. Skills we will start to develop are key to who we are growing into as adults. The first thing we start to really develop is an awareness of our strengths and weaknesses. We become conscious of what we do great and what we need to work on. As we move into our early thirties to mid-thirties, we really hone in on this to become a more complete person at home and at work. The next characteristic we will start to become aware of is the relationships we have developed over the years and the ones we are currently developing. You will see that your development and those of the relationships don't have the same energy as they did in previous years. That's because life is constantly lifing, changing our priorities, shifting our dynamics, and reshaping how we connect with the world.

For example, relationships in our thirties don't have the same feel as they did in childhood, teenage years, or even in our twenties. You will find yourself being aware of how you spend your time, with the conversations, and even time spent together. You will notice conversations change, and they are either going to be tolerable or intolerable. This is life "lifing" again, showing us that even the closest bonds shift as we grow. And the most important attribute you will become aware of is your health. Health in your thirties becomes an integral part of life, and what you do from this point when it concerns your health will stick with you for the rest of your life.

What are your strengths? What are your weaknesses? As you have developed over the past two decades, you have developed strengths, whether physical or mental. As you have developed your career goals, you have found what you are great at doing. Life be lifing, but if there's one thing we learn in our thirties, it's how to maximize those strengths to keep moving forward. You have most likely gravitated to what you do well and enhanced your ability to be efficient at it. I have always felt it important for a person to maximize their strengths.

If you are in your career, your strength has most likely helped you gain the position. I was in sales, and my strength was being able to actively listen and have great conversations. People felt comfortable with me because I listened and delivered what their needs were based on our conversation. Some strengths are in math, reading, coaching, inventory, or strategic problem-solving. In life, enhancing your strengths will help you gain knowledge and understanding. This is how you navigate when life is "lifing"—you play to your strengths, build on them, and use them to keep going.

Most people don't discuss their weaknesses because they are not proud of them. As humans, we are not perfect. We all contain imperfections. It is what makes us unique. But life will force you to confront those weaknesses. When life is "lifing," it will expose the areas you need to work on. Most employers and consultants will suggest turning your weaknesses into strengths. There is nothing wrong with working on your weaknesses. Acknowledging that you have a weakness shows strength. Make them as strong as you can, but don't consume yourself with making a weakness a strength.

My weakness in my career has always been the follow-up if the person didn't purchase from me. Early in my career, I was told if they don't buy from you "right now," they most likely bought from someone else the same day, somewhere else. I never would follow up and find out. After years of not following up, I remember a lady coming back to me and purchasing. I had spent hours with her originally—at least two to three hours. She was very undecided and wanted time to think about the purchase. She came back years later and explained to me that she ended up losing her job and never purchased from anybody. She said I impressed her by explaining the vehicle, and she said I was easy to talk to, so she was hoping I was still there. Luckily, I was, because she ended up purchasing from me that day. It was also lucky for me because it showed me that this was a weakness of mine that needed immediate attention.

How many people slipped through the cracks and just needed a follow-up call or a friendly "hello" or "how are you" call from me to earn their business? I worked on this weakness as much as I could, but I'm still not the best at following up if they didn't purchase. I was so worried about this flaw of mine that I ended up hiring an assistant from the local college, MTSU, part-time to help me follow up with unsold prospects. This was the most productive decision I could have made. My assistant helped save me time and was an incredible follow-up person. I had more unsold prospects coming in than I ever could have imagined. Improve your weaknesses so that they don't hinder you from being successful. Understanding that you have a weakness is a sign that you want to become better and more complete. Consulting with peers, coaches, and consultants are other ways to help develop your strengths and weaknesses. Never be afraid to tackle the things that make you uncomfortable. When life is "lifing," these tests will help you grow and reach your full potential.

While growing up as a child, going into your teens, and even in your twenties, you have developed special bonds and friendships with people for over a decade or even two decades. What does that look like growing into your thirties? Well, by this time, a few things have happened. You have built a career and have a work-life, some have a wife and kids, and some are still enjoying the nightlife. So what about your friends? Naturally, a few things happen—some of which are priorities, money, time, different lifestyles, and the dreaded comparison of lives.

Relationships are important, and maintaining them is very difficult. The bond in any relationship will have to be strong moving forward. There will have to be a lot of understanding, trust, and space. When you think back to childhood, there was a lot of time and space to maintain a great relationship because you spent a lot of time together, whether it was school, sports, activities, or even just in the neighborhood. The time and ability to occupy it were available. Now we have to prioritize everything every day. Availability is minimal, but you still want to keep the relationship because it is important. Where is the time? Well, it is there if the relationship is important—the time will be right in front of you. But life keeps "lifing"—priorities shift, and sometimes the relationships you cherish get less of your attention.

I have a few friends that I have maintained relationships with for 20-plus years. One of those friends I talk to normally once a day; everybody else I talk to at least two times a month, maybe a little more depending on how life is "lifing" for them. I grew up with about 20 or so friends and added a few during my journey of life. Where are they? Well, just like the name of this book—life is "lifing." It's never a scenario of a disagreement or a drag-out fight. Life gravitates you in different directions, and when it does, priorities can and will change.

For instance, my best friend in grade school, though we are still great friends, we don't talk every day. As a matter of fact, we may talk once every few months just to check on each other. It's still a strong bond between us, but he has his life with his family and friends, and I have mine with my family. It is never an uncomfortable conversation. When we do talk, we pick up right where we left off, and we may only talk for ten minutes or so, but it is always a great conversation. I am very happy for him—he is a business owner and has a very successful real estate development company in Texas.

I have other relationships that I also have to maintain besides my personal ones with my family. We also have to maintain work relationships and networking relationships. Work relationships are very important because they show that you are a fit in your workspace. They show camaraderie in the workspace. They are much easier to maintain because of two reasons. The first reason is that the conversation is normally about a topic that you know very well—WORK. Now, depending on who you have made a relationship with at work, it depends on how comfortable you are or can be with these relationships.

When I build teams, I create safe spaces to talk about whatever you want. Gaining trust in any relationship is the glue to a successful relationship. A great relationship starts with trust and builds a solid foundation from that trust. Actively listening to coworkers and peers will also help you learn about trials and tribulations that you may think you are going through alone. Trust me, you are not. This is why work relationships are so important—build, learn, and develop solutions with those you work with. This will build the entire team and brand stronger together.

I learned about building strong teams by watching one of my previous leaders and how he treated his team. Josh Potts, though he was younger than me, which is most likely what inspired me to follow him, was an amazing leader. He understood early that if you take care of your team, they will take care of you. Josh broke many records with every team he has ever managed. He picked great leaders to delegate authority. He also practiced team building and made sure his staff was having fun. He still uses the same leadership style to this day. This is the secret to his success and why his dealership is always number one in Houston, Texas, and also the country most months. He makes sure his team practices camaraderie.

Your work team is very important in your life. Some may say you will spend just as much face time with your work friends as you will with your family. So it is important that you maintain positive relationships with your peers. Continue to network with those in your field and keep those relationships improving. The relationships you keep in contact with but don't work with will be your best indicators of the career you chose. They will be your eyes and ears outside of the company that employs you. They will help you gain knowledge on salary ranges and benefits, improved processes in your field, and, of course, common struggles. This will give you the edge if you can use the information to your benefit when it comes to promotions and raises. Never be afraid to use information to negotiate your worth.

We have talked about friendships, work relationships, and networking. In most cases, you will naturally learn how to manage these relationships. All I would like to think is that we are giving you an edge on learning how to process what you are actually doing with the relationships you develop. Maintaining healthy relationships in your life can only help you achieve the greatness you already want for yourself.

I felt it was important to address the one thing that will mostly decide the true quality of life from thirty until the end. Thirty is young, but your body is starting to change. From your diet, heart rate, blood pressure, to joints and bones changing position. Being aware of your health can make your journey in life a little easier. I didn't treat my body well in my late twenties. I was a hard drinker and a heavy fried-food eater by that time. I was out of the Army and not being aware of what I was eating, nor did I acknowledge the fact that I was gaining weight fast. I was eating a lot of burgers, fries, pasta, and bread—some of the worst food you could possibly eat.

In just four years, I had gained 95 pounds. The worst part of this gain is I had not noticed it. I went from a solid 220 pounds to somewhere north of 309 pounds. You would think I would have felt it before I reached 270 or 290 pounds. I didn't even realize it until I started having short chest pains one day while driving home 16 years ago. I drove myself to the emergency room in Nashville, Tennessee. After a few blood tests, I was diagnosed with diabetes. I wasn't educated on what that was, but I was scared. I was a young 30 and experiencing an accelerated heartbeat along with feeling sluggish. I thought it was a heart attack. They gave me some medicine and a follow-up the next day with my doctor.

The next day, I took off work and went to my appointment. The doctor explained everything about diabetes. She told me all of the signs and symptoms of not controlling my diet and exercise—losing limbs, failing organs, blurred vision, and even leading to blindness. She also told me that it can be reversed. She explained that if I managed my diet and exercise, I wouldn't have to suffer from this forever. My new priority was my health. It was more important than money to me. I did research on how to lose weight and manage diabetes. I worked very hard to manage my weight and sugar levels.

Within the first year and a half, I had lost 75 to 80 pounds. I was looking and feeling a lot better. My doctor was very happy with my progress. I was doing so well that they actually took me off the medicine when I was 38 years old. I was back on the medicine by 43. Life be lifing like that—you think you're in the clear, and suddenly you're not. You have to stay on top of your diet at all times. This was a scary time for me. I am very grateful to my doctor for the encouragement and education to help me manage this illness.

The first step to maintaining great health is education. Be aware of your body and what you are doing with it. Never overindulge in anything because it could lead to a costly consequence. While in our twenties, we have a great time, but by the time we hit our thirties, we could be feeling some of the effects from previous decades. I had a great friend who developed very bad knee pain by his mid-thirties because he played football, and his knees had been under too much pressure by the time he hit his thirties. He ended up getting both knees replaced before he was forty.

Of course, it isn't all bad—most people's health in their thirties is great and will be fine. But remember, your quality of life will depend on how you treat your body moving forward.

As we walk out of our thirties and move into our forties, there are many valuable lessons we have learned. Many of them deal with the development of relationships, strengths and weaknesses, and, of course, health. We have looked inside ourselves to find how to make our strengths stronger and how to ensure our weaknesses don't hinder our progress in life. We have learned to have awareness of our health and be aware of our body. Being aware in all of these scenarios puts you ahead of the average person. Taking these attributes and applying them as you move into your forties prepares you for what is to come in the future. All three of these will help you become the best version of YOU.

THE FORTIES

The real fun begins right here in the forties. We are in a different stage of life. We are focused on mastering finances, continuing education, and valuing life. It is amazing how far we have come in our developmental stages over the past four decades. At this point in life, we are reaping what we have been working so hard to accomplish. This is an era of fulfillment. No matter what career you have chosen, at this point you are vested in continuing knowledge of the career so that you can maximize your potential. You should be thinking about the road to retirement and making plans to accomplish it. Most of all, we are valuing how far we have come in life, focusing on family, relationships, and time. Some call it a mid-life crisis; I call it Adult Lifing.

The real question is, what does it mean to master finances? This isn't an easy task, especially if you haven't started saving by now, but it's not too late to start. It's all about taking the first step. Life has been lifing, and maybe you didn't get the perfect financial start you hoped for, but taking the first step now still matters. Ever heard the statement "The more you make, the more you spend"? It's true—the more you make, the more opportunity you have to spend. Money can put you in a different budgeting bracket. This is why it is so important to pay yourself as much and as often as possible. In most cases, people use their job as their savings through stock options, a 401(k), or a pension. That's great if you've been doing it for years and have a portfolio growing over time, but Life Be Lifing, and not everyone's journey is the same.

According to studies, the median 40-year-old has about $7,500 saved. This is not enough to retire, but it's a start, and depending on salary and obligations, you can build this into a small fortune before you retire. No matter how much you make, it's always helpful to consult with a financial planner who can educate you on how to make your money work for you. I remember talking to my financial advisor years ago, asking him how I was supposed to save all this money for retirement. He gave me some solid advice, reminding me to be careful with my splurging. The key, he said, was in small choices: never buy anything once that you can't afford twice. That little nugget of wisdom has probably saved me hundreds of thousands over the years. Life be lifing, and it can lead you to financial surprises if you don't plan ahead.

He also educated me on credit card cash back and how I should always send that money to my savings account. He did say to be careful because of interest, but the one thing he told me that made a lot of sense was that gifted money should always be saved. He said if you get birthday or Christmas money, then save it. All the money adds up in the end. Another tool I used to save was sending my change from my check to my savings. That is a helpful tool my bank offers that usually adds up over the years. I am not a financial planner, so I wouldn't dare try to give financial advice, but I definitely pay attention to any little helpful hints to put money away for retirement and for a rainy day.

Another form of equity is real estate. It is important to have some type of real estate. Whether you own a piece of property, a home, or farmland, real estate normally goes up in value and will help your net worth over time. But most importantly, never be afraid to invest in yourself. When you invest in things you enjoy doing, you never really work a day in your life. Mastering finances in your forties sets you up for the future when you can focus on living life rather than chasing it.

Once you have hit your forties, you have already started the process of mastering your career. Depending on how you started your career, most likely by this time many changes have occurred over time. No matter how great you are at any profession, the process will always change to make it more efficient. The problem happens when, while you are still on the old process, the twenty-year-olds are learning the new way. What I have tried to show you through this process is that we are life learners. We have to continue, now more than ever, to learn and adapt to new concepts and ideas.

When I started in sales over 20 years ago, there was a lot of paperwork and banking relationships. There was very little internet or computer interaction. Prospecting was done with mailing and phone calls. This process was real basic and easy to follow. Over time, this process has changed, and with change comes adapting. One of the hardest things to do is to change a process that you have mastered. The first line of defense is always, "Why is this process changing?" Most likely, it is changing because a new method has proven to be more efficient. Before any company will change a process that is working for them, they have most likely found research that shows this is now the best way to do business.

Before I knew it, they had installed a program for us to keep up with customers in a database, they required us to get emails from every customer, and they had installed an online way to buy cars. This all happened within my first 10 years in the industry. These were all processes that had changed the industry dramatically. The new way of selling cars went from AutoTrader magazines to online sales. This was not only amazing to watch but hard to adapt to at first. It was like learning the process all over again. I was lost for a couple of days trying to figure out this internet process and how to communicate through email to talk to customers. I watched old salespeople get so frustrated that they either retired or quit. It was too much change for them to bear.

Another part of the process that changed was financing companies that financed the vehicles. Instead of calling the bank and building bank relationships, which was the way we had always done, it had now changed to going through a computer system. While going through the computer, the credit has to score. If it doesn't score, you can't call the bank to get an approval. It changed the industry. Those of us that were able to adapt became more successful. Embracing change is what will give you the competitive edge in your industry.

Continuing education and keeping up with the new technology and development in your industry will guarantee long-term success. Gaining certifications and leadership certifications is also a great way to continue growing. I always take advantage of the opportunity to learn new concepts and ideas. At first, my mind naturally blocks the new idea or concept, but I have a way of reasoning with myself and showing myself that this is the logical solution to helping more people. I feel once we understand a new idea or a new way of doing business—really understand it by practicing it and making it a part of our new process—the results will shine.

In your forties, you are likely creating space for what is important to you. This is the time when you start valuing life in a different way. You've put in the work, and now you're enjoying the fruits of your labor. The career that once seemed so demanding has provided stability, and you can now focus on family, relationships, and time. Of course, you remember the ripples it took to get to this stage. The pain, the sweat, and the tears you fought to become who you are today. You look back at all the sacrifices and challenges and appreciate how far you've come. It wasn't always easy because, as we know, life be lifing—it throws unexpected hurdles your way, but every step has been a learning process, and now you're able to see the bigger picture.

I can remember my very first day at Jim Reed Chevrolet. I didn't even realize then that it was the first day of my career. I watched the managers, the customers, and the hustle of the place. At the end of the day, everyone seemed happy—even the customers. I didn't sell anything that day, but I learned that I wanted to be part of it. Twenty-plus years later, I did it. I fit in, and I'm sure you're doing the same in your career now. Life has been lifing since day one, but we've managed to carve out our place in it.

So what does valuing life in your forties really mean? It means appreciating everything you've been through, even the struggles. The good times were easy, but the hard times gave you the strength and wisdom to get where you are today. By the time we hit our forties, our awareness of ourselves is high, our knowledge is high, and, of course, our benefits are high. You have made it this far because you have overcome so much that tried to block you from being successful. Think about your own story. How many obstacles stood in your way up to this point? What did you do to overcome those obstacles? What did you learn? Did you have to learn the same lesson again? Valuing life is appreciating those experiences. It's also about benefiting from those experiences. It means it's finally time for you to focus on what matters most: family, friends, health, and quality time; if that wasn't your focus before. It's about learning to balance work with life and taking time to enjoy the moments, because life will keep lifing, and it's up to you to appreciate what you've built along the way.

It tends to be a little scary to get comfortable. It helps us grow into the future us, into our fifties and beyond to retirement. All of these developmental skills we have learned over the past four decades have gotten us to this point where we can start to appreciate the fact that within two decades, we can retire. I know what you're thinking: RETIREMENT, I'm only forty-something. It's never too early to prepare for retirement. Mentally and financially, it takes time to prepare to slow down and pace yourself for the future. A lot of times, people feel success is only monetary. Throughout this entire book, your success has never depended on money. Success is not just about the money in your bank account—it's about the experiences, the relationships, and the lessons learned along the way. Life has been lifing all along, and through it all, you've gained invaluable experience that no paycheck can replace. Always remember, you can maintain a budget, you can find another job if needed, but you can never replace the journey of experiencing life itself.

LIFE

The beauty of life lies in the simple truth that every single day is an opportunity—a chance to start fresh, to correct our course, and to live in alignment with our truth. Every day offers a renewed opportunity to step closer to our purpose. The only real challenge is resisting the weight of negativity. Stay focused, stay positive, and remember that the life you want is within reach—if you're willing to work for it. Growth doesn't come from staying comfortable. It comes from pushing boundaries, from stepping into situations that challenge us to evolve.

If at any point you feel lost, like you're not navigating toward your true purpose, remember this: it's never too late to reinvent yourself. Reinvention is not a sign of failure but a testament to your strength. I remember sitting in a training seminar in the mid-2000s, watching the speaker captivate the room. I wasn't just listening to his words—I was absorbing the energy he created, the power he had over the room. I remember thinking, I could do this. I can be up there. I can teach and inspire people. That moment sparked something in me. My mother had taught for 40 years, and in that instant, I understood her passion. She wasn't just imparting knowledge; she was changing lives. I wanted that too.

But the moment I spoke my dream aloud, I was met with skepticism. I remember the laughter and doubt when I told my colleagues I wanted to be a speaker. That doubt wasn't just from them—it was in me too. But here's the truth about doubt: it's not there to stop you; it's there to be crushed. I knew that to turn my vision into reality, I had to change. Not just a little—I had to transform my entire mindset, my habits, my image. I had to evolve into the person I needed to be. And I knew it wasn't going to happen overnight. At that time, I didn't have the knowledge or experience to back up my ambition. But that didn't stop me. It fueled me.

I immersed myself in learning—about myself, my craft, and the world around me. With every step, my confidence grew, and the path to my goal became clearer. When I finally stepped into my purpose as a consultant and speaker, it felt like coming home. It wasn't just a career move; it was a soul move. It filled me in a way no paycheck or title ever could. I realized then that true fulfillment comes from walking in your purpose, from knowing that you are living the life you were meant to live.

Here's the thing: no dream is too small. If it's in your heart, it's there for a reason. Your dreams are your guideposts, leading you to your highest self. Don't let anyone, not even yourself, tell you they're impossible. The only thing standing between you and what you want is the work you're willing to put in. In life, you have to dream big, set goals, and work relentlessly to achieve them. Obstacles will come—they always do. But they're not roadblocks; they're tests. Tests to see how bad you want it. And when you feel like giving up, remember: you're closer than you think.

As Nike says: Just Do It. Because if you don't, no one else will do it for you. Your life is in your hands. Your success, your happiness, your fulfillment—they all come from your decisions, your effort, and your determination to never settle for anything less than your best.

BECAUSE LIFE BE LIFING

Life doesn't pause for us. It doesn't slow down when we're overwhelmed or stop when we're unprepared. Life is always moving, always shifting, always happening—whether we're ready for it or not. This is what we mean when we say, Life is Lifing. It's a simple phrase that captures the relentless pace, the constant changes, and the inevitable ups and downs of our journey. It's a reminder that life isn't something we can always control, but it's something we can always navigate.

The entire purpose of this book has been to equip you with the mindset and tools to face life head-on, no matter what stage you're in. From our twenties, where we're just starting to build, to our forties, where we're reaping what we've sown, and beyond—it's about understanding that life doesn't give us a break just because we've had enough. But here's the beauty: it doesn't need to. Because while life is busy doing its thing—Lifing—we're busy growing, learning, and evolving. And through every challenge, setback, and triumph, we're becoming who we're meant to be.

This idea—that life is constantly moving—means we must keep moving too. There's no such thing as staying still. Even in those moments when we feel stagnant, we're growing beneath the surface, whether we realize it or not. Every failure teaches us something. Every heartbreak reshapes us. Every success shows us what's possible. The goal isn't to avoid life's challenges—it's to embrace them. To understand that when life is Lifing, it's doing exactly what it's supposed to do: pushing us, testing us, and shaping us into stronger, wiser, more fulfilled individuals.

When we accept that life doesn't follow our plan, we become more flexible, more resilient. We learn to pivot, to adapt, and to thrive in whatever circumstances we find ourselves in. Because Life is Lifing doesn't just mean that life is unpredictable—it means that life is rich. It's full of experiences, lessons, and opportunities to grow. It's not always easy, but it's always worth it.

Think about all the times life didn't go the way you planned. Think about the moments where everything seemed to fall apart, where you couldn't see a way forward. Now think about where you are now. You survived. You adapted. You found new ways to move forward. That's what life does. It forces us to discover strengths we didn't know we had. It pushes us to reinvent ourselves, to adjust our dreams, and to keep going, even when it feels impossible.

This is the thread that ties every chapter in this book together: the understanding that life will always throw challenges our way, but how we respond to those challenges defines who we are. It's the choices we make when things get tough that shape the course of our lives. It's the decision to keep going when we want to quit. It's the courage to dream bigger when life tells us to play small. And it's the resilience to get back up, time and time again, no matter how many times we fall.

We've talked about mastering finances, building careers, nurturing relationships, and valuing our lives. But underneath all of that is this simple truth: Life is Lifing, and the only way to truly succeed is to embrace it. Not fight it. Not resist it. But flow with it. Trust the process, even when it's messy. Trust yourself, even when you feel unsure. Trust that every experience—good or bad—is shaping you into the person you're meant to be.

As we move through life, we'll encounter new stages, new goals, and new dreams. We'll face different kinds of challenges and victories. But the one constant is that life will keep moving.

It will keep lifing. And so will we. With every chapter, with every lesson, we become more equipped to face the next stage of life with grace, strength, and purpose.

So, when life is lifing—when it feels like everything is happening at once, when you're faced with more than you think you can handle—remember that you've been here before. You've faced uncertainty, fear, and doubt. And you've come through stronger every time. This is just another part of the journey. Another lesson. Another opportunity to grow.

Because, in the end, life is lifing isn't a problem to solve. It's a gift. A gift of constant growth, constant evolution, and constant opportunity to become the best version of ourselves. It's a reminder that no matter what, we have the power to navigate our way through. We have the strength to keep going. We have the courage to keep growing.

And that's what makes life beautiful.

ABOUT THE AUTHOR

Emery J. Cannon, CPC, is the founder of Cannon Sales Consulting LLC, a premier sales training and consulting firm specializing in helping individuals and organizations achieve peak sales performance. With over a decade of experience in coaching and sales strategy, Emery has built a reputation for empowering professionals to drive results through his personalized, hands-on approach. His company, Cannon Sales Consulting (cannonsalestraining.com), offers a variety of services designed to optimize sales techniques, leadership skills, and business growth.

In 2024, Emery released his highly anticipated first book, It's Not Rocket Science...It's Sales, where he shares practical insights and proven methods to excel in the world of sales. The book offers readers a comprehensive guide to mastering sales fundamentals, with actionable strategies for success in today's competitive market.

A Certified Professional Coach, Emery integrates his expertise in personal development, emotional intelligence, and mental resilience into his coaching, allowing clients to achieve both professional and personal breakthroughs.

For more information or to connect with Emery J Cannon, CPC, visit Cannon Sales Consulting LLC or follow him on social media:

Address:
Cannon Sales Consulting LLC
103 S Florissant Rd, Ferguson MO 63135
Website: www.cannonsalestraining.com

Social Media:
Facebook: Cannon Sales Consulting
LinkedIn: Coach Emery Cannon CPC
YouTube: Coach Emery Cannon CPC
TikTok: Coach Cannon CPC
Google: Search for "Emery Cannon CPC" or "Coach Emery Cannon"

Made in the USA
Columbia, SC
17 October 2024